My Spirit Rejoices

Through the Year with Mary

AGNES KOVACS

the WORD
among us
Press

This book was published by The Word Among Us. Since 1981, The Word Among Us has been answering the call of the Second Vatican Council to help Catholic laypeople encounter Christ in the Scriptures.

The name of our company comes from the prologue to the Gospel of John and reflects the vision and purpose of all of our publications: to be an instrument of the Spirit, whose desire is to manifest Jesus' presence in and to the children of God. In this way, we hope to contribute to the Church's ongoing mission of proclaiming the gospel to the world so that all people would know the love and mercy of our Lord and grow more deeply in their faith as missionary disciples.

Our monthly devotional magazine, *The Word Among Us*, features meditations on the daily and Sunday Mass readings and currently reaches more than one million Catholics in North America and another half-million Catholics in one hundred countries around the world. Our book division, The Word Among Us Press, publishes numerous books, Bible studies, and pamphlets that help Catholics grow in their faith.

To learn more about who we are and what we publish, visit us at www.wau.org. There you will find a variety of Catholic resources that will help you grow in your faith.

Embrace His Word, Listen to God . . .

www.wau.org

Messages for Each Day of the Year
Perpetual Calendars

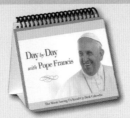

**The Catholic Mom's
Desk Calendar**
Item# CMOME7

**Day by Day with
Pope Francis**
Item# CPFDE5

**Fr. Larry Richards'
Scripture Desk Calendar**
Item# CNBNE4

Introduction

The Scriptures say very little about Mary of Nazareth, the mother of Jesus. Yet she has inspired the Christian imagination from apostolic times to our days. Devotion to her influenced and shaped the teachings of the Church, leading to a strand of theology in its own right, Mariology.

Apparitions of Mary dot the devotional landscapes of the centuries. She has been a favorite subject of artists, poets, and popes. Her appeal is reflected in the multitude of names and titles associated with her, in countries and continents selecting her as patroness, and in the countless ways she has become part of the fabric of human experience.

What has drawn diverse peoples to Mary throughout the ages? What attracts us to her in our own times?

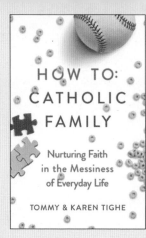

How To: Catholic Family
Nurturing Faith in the Messiness of Everyday Life

This book is a practical, encouraging guide for Catholic parents who want to impart the faith to their children but aren't quite sure where to start. Topics include leading by example, having conversations about faith, reading the Bible as a family, praying together, learning about the saints, understanding what the Mass means, celebrating special feast days, and finding community with other Catholic families.

With humor, Tommy and Karen Tighe let readers know that there will be plenty of "fails" along the way, but also encourage them not to give up trying to develop a faith-filled family life.

160 pages, 5¼ x 8, Item# BFAME9

As I pondered these questions, I came to realize that Mary of Nazareth, the Blessed Mother, defies all singular descriptions and visual representations. Our image of her is shaped not only by God's word and the teachings of the Church but also by our life experiences, in which we find a connection to her fully human life. She was a child, friend, spouse, parent, and disciple. She lived the gamut of feelings and emotions that mark our days. She comes clothed in our symbols and embodying our identities.

Yet Mary was a unique human being, chosen by God for a special role in salvation history. This push and pull of familiarity and otherness creates a continuum on which we may connect to Our Lady. Where we find ourselves on this continuum may change as we are changed by our Christian journey.

The pages that follow offer a glimpse into how people of faith throughout the centuries, in the Christian East and West, expressed their connection to and

Call Me Blessed

Get to know the women of the Bible, whose stories bring to life the dignity and vocation of women throughout the ages. Consider the stories of these women in the light of the gospel, and see how their truths beckon you to also grow as a woman of God.

160 pages, 7 x 10, Item# JPF1E8

Better Together

God has a lot to say about Christians gathering together in friendship. This beautifully designed Scripture study and journal explores God's plan for his people together. There are inspiring reflections and tangible tools for extending gracious hospitality that builds meaningful relationships.

144 pages, 7 x 10, Item# JPF2E9

Order online at wau.org/bookstore or call 1-800-775-WORD

beliefs about Mary of Nazareth. Selected quotes are accompanied by images of Mary, inviting us to tap into the Church's rich tradition and thus broaden our own appreciation for the many faces of Mary.

Among my favorite Scripture passages are the opening verses of the Magnificat: "My soul proclaims the greatness of the Lord; my spirit rejoices in God my savior" (Luke 1:46-47). May Mary's song of praise become ours as we walk with her day by day; may our spirits rejoice!

—AGNES M. KOVACS

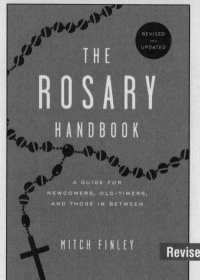

Theotokos of the Holy Protection
Marek Czarnecki

January

About the Author

Agnes M. Kovacs, a native of Hungary, has lived in the United States for thirty years. She is a daughter, sister, aunt, wife, mother, and grandmother who cherishes the relationships with her large, extended family spanning multiple continents. Prayer, as first modeled in her family of origin and then practiced in different cultural contexts, has been a cornerstone of Agnes' life of faith. She enjoys exploring different prayer forms, both in personal and communal prayer. Agnes currently serves as director of continuing formation at Saint Meinrad Seminary and School of Theology.

The Virgin Mary, who at the message of the angel received the Word of God in her heart and in her body and gave Life to the world, is acknowledged and honored as being truly the Mother of God.

—*Lumen Gentium*

Mary, Mother of God
JANUARY 1

May the Blessed Virgin revive in us the ardent "desire to live in grace," to persevere in the grace of God.

—Pope St. John Paul II

DECEMBER 31

Blessed are you, Mary, who have borne in your womb the Mighty One, who in his power bears the world and governs all.

—**Balai the Syrian**

JANUARY 2

The ultimate meaning of the Immaculate Conception lies not in Mary, but in God's wish to become incarnate. God determines to communicate the divine self totally. God prepares a living temple as a dwelling place. God enters it, assumes it, and renders it divine.

—**Leonardo Boff**

DECEMBER 30

When eight days were completed for his circumcision, he was named Jesus, the name given him by the angel before he was conceived in the womb.

—Luke 2:21

Most Holy Name of Jesus
JANUARY 3

There is an infinite distance between Marian veneration and worship of the Trinity and the Incarnate Word.

—Pope St. John Paul II

DECEMBER 29

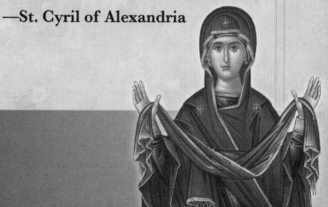

L et us fear and worship the undivided Trinity as we sing the praise of the ever-virgin Mary, the holy temple of God, and of God himself, her Son and spotless Bridegroom.

—**St. Cyril of Alexandria**

JANUARY 4

Mirror of justice,
preserve in us
the love of divine grace,
so that living humbly and happily
in obedience to our Christian calling,
we may always enjoy
the Lord's friendship
and your motherly consolation.

—Pope St. John XXIII

DECEMBER 28

May Mary, the Mother of God and our tender Mother, support us always, that we may remain faithful to our Christian vocation and be able to realize the aspiration for justice and peace that we carry within us at the start of this new year.

—**Pope Francis**

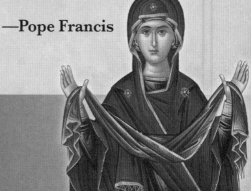

JANUARY 5

This mystery—the Incarnation of the Word and the divine Motherhood of Mary—is great and certainly far from easy to understand with the human mind alone.

—Pope Benedict XVI

DECEMBER 27

Jesus . . . is the Son of God, he is generated by God and *at the same time* he is the son of a woman, Mary. He comes from her. He is *of* God and *of* Mary.

For this reason one can and must call the Mother of Jesus the Mother of God, . . . [a] title, rendered in Greek as *Theotokos*.

—**Pope Benedict XVI**

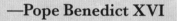

Blest in the message Gabriel brought;
Blest in the work the Spirit wrought;
Most blest, to bring to human birth
The long desired of all the earth.

—Venantius Fortunatus

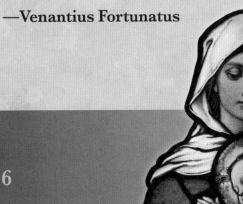

DECEMBER 26

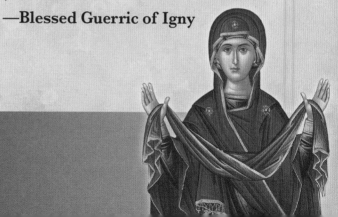

She is the Mother of the Life from whom all men take life: in giving birth to this life herself, she has somehow given rebirth to all those who have lived it. Only one was begotten, but we have all been reborn.

—Blessed Guerric of Igny

JANUARY 7

May Mary help us to recognize in the face of the Child of Bethlehem, conceived in her virginal womb, the divine Redeemer who came into the world to reveal to us the authentic face of God.

—Pope Benedict XVI

Birth of Jesus Christ
DECEMBER 25

As Mother of God and mother of all God's children, Mary is exalted above all creatures on the throne of glory.

—St. Teresa Benedicta of the Cross

JANUARY 8

I f you reverence the truth, give thanks to the Virgin since from the ground of her virgin flesh has arisen the Truth which you worship.

—St. Bernard of Clairvaux

DECEMBER 24

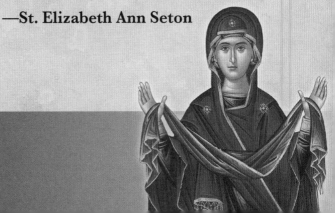

Mary *full of grace—Mother of Jesus!* We love and honor our Jesus when we love and honor her. . . . Our best honor to Mary is the imitation of her virtues—her life a model for all conditions of life.

—St. Elizabeth Ann Seton

JANUARY 9

Let us . . . allow her to accompany us; may her sentiments prompt us to prepare ourselves with heartfelt sincerity and openness of spirit to recognize in the Child of Bethlehem the Son of God who came into the world for our redemption.

—Pope Benedict XVI

DECEMBER 23

Blessed and revered may you be, my Lady, O Virgin Mary, most holy Mother of God. You are, in truth, his best creation; and no one has ever loved him so intimately as you, O glorious Lady.

—St. Bridget of Sweden

JANUARY 10

The Virgin's maternal intercession, her exemplary holiness and the divine grace which is in her became for the human race a reason for divine hope.

—Pope St. Paul VI

DECEMBER 22

May the Mother of God . . . teach us to welcome God made man, so that every year, every month, every day may be filled with his eternal Love. So be it!

—Pope Francis

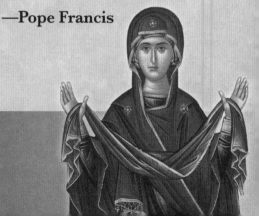

JANUARY 11

O Christ,
O blessed is the Virgin, your Mother. . . .

To us, who do not cease to extol

her virginal conception,

give us, we pray you,

the ability to reach with pure heart

the solemnity of your Birth.

—Seventh-century prayer

DECEMBER 21

One cannot contemplate Mary without being attracted by Christ, and one cannot look at Christ without immediately perceiving the presence of Mary.

—Pope Benedict XVI

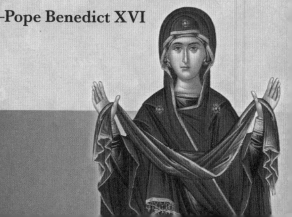

JANUARY 12

Arise in faith, hasten in devotion, open in praise and thanksgiving. *Behold the handmaid of the Lord,* she says, *be it done to me according to your word.*

—St. Bernard of Clairvaux

DECEMBER 20

For every man who is born again, the water of baptism is like the virginal womb. The same Spirit that filled the Virgin now fills the baptismal font.

—St. Leo the Great

JANUARY 13

Again and again
She comes into our lives,
into the life of the world,
to bring joy and peace.
To lead us back to God.

—St. Teresa of Calcutta

DECEMBER 19

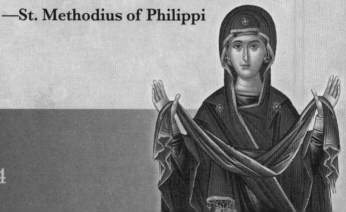

O holy Mother of God, remember us, I say, who make our boast in you and who in august hymns celebrate the memory, which will ever live, and never fade away.

—St. Methodius of Philippi

JANUARY 14

She becomes also—by association with her Son—the sign of contradiction to the world and, at the same time, the sign of hope whom all generations shall call blessed.

—**Pope St. John Paul II**

DECEMBER 18

By the power of your prayers, O Mother of the Most High, may God give the world and its inhabitants the fullness of peace!

—Balai the Syrian

JANUARY 15

May the light of the Virgin and the grace of the Lamb be our inheritance in their everlasting abode.

—Tadhg Gaelach

DECEMBER 17

I t is theologically and anthropologically important for women to be at the center of Christianity. Through Mary, and the other holy women, the feminine element stands at the heart of the Christian religion.

—Pope Benedict XVI

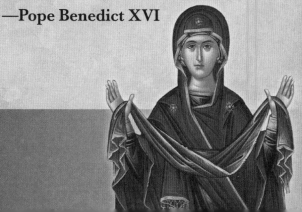

JANUARY 16

Mary is a woman of hope: only because she believes in God's promises and awaits the salvation of Israel can the angel visit her and call her to the decisive service of these promises.

—Pope Benedict XVI

DECEMBER 16

In honoring Mary, in every thought of her, we do homage to the superabundant mercy and love of the Redeemer.

—Venerable Pope Pius XII

JANUARY 17

To profess that Mary is full of grace is to admit that God—as goodness, gentleness, joy, righteousness, balance, transparency, freedom, and exuberance in all of life's dimensions—has given the divine self totally to this simple woman of the people.

—**Leonardo Boff**

DECEMBER 15

When I sinned against the Son, I distressed the Mother; nor could I have offended the Mother without injuring the Son.

—**St. Anselm of Canterbury**

JANUARY 18

Today, [Our Lady of Guadalupe] continues to make her presence known in an intimate, consoling way to every devotee who calls out her name.

—Jeanette Rodriguez

DECEMBER 14

Mary is the Bow of the morning, wherein are stored the treasures of Heaven. And from her God shined forth upon us; and of her the Prophets foretold.

—Rabbula, Syriac bishop

JANUARY 19

May we who rejoice in Our Lady of Guadalupe live united and at peace in this world until the day of the Lord dawns in glory.

—Prayer after Communion for the
Feast of Our Lady of Guadalupe

DECEMBER 13

Only Mary contains him whom the world can never contain. Only Mary carries in her arms the One who carries the world. And only Mary generated her creator and nourished the One who nourishes the living.

—**St. Peter Chrysologus**

JANUARY 20

O God, . . . grant that all who invoke the Blessed Virgin of Guadalupe, may seek with ever more lively faith the progress of peoples in the ways of justice and of peace.

—Collect for the Feast of Our Lady of Guadalupe

Our Lady of Guadalupe
DECEMBER 12

She who physically gave Jesus to the world wants nothing more than to see him living spiritually in the world today among Christians.

—**Chiara Lubich**

JANUARY 21

Of course, to believe that Mary, by mystery's design, is without sin is not to believe that her life was a bed of roses. . . . To say that she is immaculate does not mean that she did not suffer, that she was never troubled, or that she had no need for faith and hope.

—Leonardo Boff

DECEMBER 11

Commemorating our most holy, pure, blessed, and glorious Lady, the Theotokos and ever-virgin Mary, with all the saints, let us commend ourselves and one another and our whole life to Christ our God.

—The Divine Liturgy of St. John Chrysostom

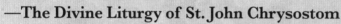

JANUARY 22

Who could be a better "Star of Hope" for us than Mary? With her "yes," with the generous offering of freedom received from the Creator, she enabled the hope of the millennia to become reality, to enter this world and its history.

—**Pope Benedict XVI**

DECEMBER 10

Glory be to the Father
Who sent the Only-begotten,
And He shined forth from Mary,
And delivered us from error,
And magnified her memorial
In heaven and on earth.

—**Balai the Syrian**

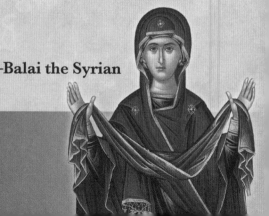

JANUARY 23

Teach us, Mary, to believe, to hope, to love with you; show us the way that leads to peace, the way to the Kingdom of Jesus. You, Star of Hope, who wait for us anxiously in the everlasting light of the eternal Homeland, shine upon us and guide us through daily events, now and at the hour of our death. Amen!

—Pope Benedict XVI

DECEMBER 9

God, who became present here on earth, truly dwells in Mary. Mary becomes his tent. What all the cultures desire—that God dwell among us—is brought about here.

—Pope Benedict XVI

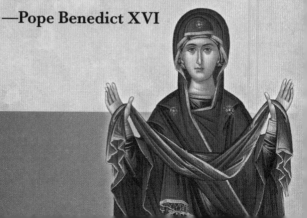

JANUARY 24

B y contemplating our beautiful Immaculate Mother, let us also recognize our truest destiny, our deepest vocation: to be loved, to be transformed by love, to be transformed by the beauty of God.

—**Pope Francis**

Immaculate Conception
DECEMBER 8

The Virgin . . . treasures in her heart the words that come from God and, piecing them together as in a mosaic, learns to understand them.

—Pope Benedict XVI

JANUARY 25

Just as the Virgin Mother pondered in her heart on the Word made flesh, so every individual soul and the entire Church are called during their earthly pilgrimage to wait for Christ who comes and to welcome him with faith and love ever new.

—Pope Benedict XVI

DECEMBER 7

He whom the entire universe could not contain was contained within your womb, O Theotokos.

—Ancient liturgical hymn

JANUARY 26

In her the Word of God chose to be silent for the season measured by God. She, too, was silent; in her the light of the world shone in darkness.

—**Caryll Houselander**

DECEMBER 6

Mary's task as Mother of God and mother of humans has always been to lead her human children to her divine Son. This she has done through the centuries, this she will do through the coming centuries until the day of the second coming of the Lord.

—Catherine de Hueck Doherty

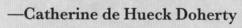

Joy must always be shared. Joy must be communicated. Mary went without delay to communicate her joy to her cousin Elizabeth. . . . This is the real commitment of Advent: to bring joy to others. Joy is the true gift of Christmas.

—**Pope Benedict XVI**

DECEMBER 5

Just as sailors are directed to port by means of a star of the sea, so Christians are directed by means of Mary to glory.

—**St. Thomas Aquinas**

JANUARY 28

Mary tells us why church buildings exist: they exist so that room may be made within us for the Word of God; so that within us and through us the Word may also be made flesh today.

—Pope Benedict XVI

DECEMBER 4

Hail to You from all! O holy one, Mary, Mother of God:
Excellent and precious Treasure of all the habitable world:
Lamp brightly shining:
Mansion of the Incomprehensible:
Pure Sanctuary of the Creator of all creatures.
Hail, through You was announced He who took away
the sin of the world and redeemed it.

—Rabbula, Syriac bishop

JANUARY 29

It is Mary who tells us what Advent is: going forth to meet the Lord who comes to meet us; waiting for him, listening to him, looking at him.

—**Pope Benedict XVI**

DECEMBER 3

At a crucial time in history, Mary offered herself, her body and soul, to God as a dwelling place. In her and from her the Son of God took flesh. Through her the Word was made flesh (cf. John 1:14).

—**Pope Benedict XVI**

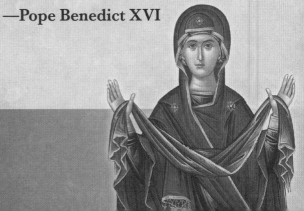

JANUARY 30

Lady, whose smiles are full of counsel and theology,
Never have you withheld those seas of light
Whose surf confounds the keenest eye.
Grace me to be the soldier of your Scotus,
Arming my actions with the news
Of your Immaculate command.

—**Thomas Merton**

DECEMBER 2

In her brief historical life, . . . the history of the whole world is concentrated, particularly the lives of all the common people of the world, who often do not know themselves that they are Christbearers.

—Caryll Houselander

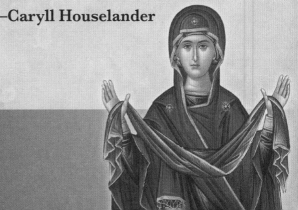

JANUARY 31

M ary sustains our journey toward Christmas, for she teaches us how to live this Advent Season in expectation of the Lord.

—**Pope Francis**

DECEMBER 1

The Rest on the Flight into Egypt
Gerard David

February

Mother Mary

December

The Mother of God, the most pure Virgin, carried the true light in her arms and brought him to those who lay in darkness.

—**St. Sophronius**

FEBRUARY 1

In Mary, the church holds up and admires the most excellent fruit of the redemption, and joyfully contemplates, as in a faultless image, that which she herself desires and hopes wholly to be.

—*Sacrosanctum Concilium*

NOVEMBER 30

Simeon blessed them and said to Mary his mother, "Behold, this child is destined for the fall and rise of many in Israel, and to be a sign that will be contradicted (and you yourself a sword will pierce) so that the thoughts of many hearts may be revealed."

—Luke 2:34-35

Presentation of the Lord
FEBRUARY 2

In celebrating this annual cycle of Christ's mysteries, Church honors with special love Mary, the Mother of God, who is joined by an inseparable bond to the saving work of her Son.

—*Sacrosanctum Concilium*

NOVEMBER 29

Hail, O Theotokos Virgin full of grace: for from thee has shone forth the Sun of righteousness, Christ our God, giving light to those in darkness.

—Great Vespers of the Presentation of the Lord

FEBRUARY 3

Through her, . . . the Reconciler of hearts and consciences—her Son, the God-man Jesus Christ—was to transform the human condition and, by his death and Resurrection, uplift the entire human family.

—**Pope St. John Paul II**

NOVEMBER 28

Our Lady's love is like a stream that has its source in the Eternal Fountains, quenches the thirst of all, can never be drained, and ever flows back to its Source.

—St. Margaret Bourgeoys

FEBRUARY 4

O mother of great mercy, deign to look with your benign eyes on me as I place my body, soul, spirit and thoughts under your protection, so that they may please your beloved Son and yourself.

—Eighteenth-century Irish prayer

NOVEMBER 27

Dearest Mother, please look on your people, who confidently honor you as their mother, longing for your help and consolation. Bless us in your heart, comfort us in our pains, stand by us in all distress, show us Jesus after our death.

—St. Hildegard of Bingen

FEBRUARY 5

The Son is the Word and she is the letter, as we said, by which forgiveness was sent forth to the whole world.

—Jacob of Serug

NOVEMBER 26

V irgin Mother of the divine offspring, through
your Son, your only child who stooped to become
brother of humankind, you are the true mother of
us all.

—St. Gertrude the Great

Mary is . . . the one who obtained mercy in a particular and exceptional way, as no other person has.

—Pope St. John Paul II

NOVEMBER 25

C ling to His most sweet Mother, who carried a Son Whom the heavens could not contain.

—St. Clare of Assisi

FEBRUARY 7

She knows the difficulties of woman—she is a woman who has suffered much hardship; all women love Mary in whose hands is mercy.

—*Lucerna Fidelium*, **an Irish devotional**

NOVEMBER 24

The Christian who does not feel that the Virgin Mary is his or her mother is an orphan.

—**Pope Francis**

FEBRUARY 8

The Son will listen to His Mother, and the Father to the Son. Little children, she is the ladder for sinners, she is the great ground of my confidence, she is the entire basis of my hope.

—St. Bernard of Clairvaux

NOVEMBER 23

On Mary's motherly face Christians recognize a most particular expression of the merciful love of God, who with the mediation of a maternal presence has us better understand the Father's own care and goodness.

—**Pope St. John Paul II**

Merciful, forgiving one who has the grace of the pure Spirit, join us in entreating the just-judging King on behalf of His fair fragrant children.

—St. Columcille of Iona

NOVEMBER 22

She has given us so many proofs that she cares for us like a Mother.

—St. Thérèse of Lisieux

FEBRUARY 10

Through your mercies, O Lord, and by the intercession of the ever pure and Blessed Virgin, may this Presentation of Mary contribute to our peace in this life and happiness in the next.

—Nineteenth-century prayer

Presentation of Mary
NOVEMBER 21

In presenting herself to Bernadette as the Immaculate Conception, Mary Most Holy came to remind the modern world, which was in danger of forgetting it, of the primacy of divine grace which is stronger than sin and death.

—**Pope Benedict XVI**

Our Lady of Lourdes
FEBRUARY 11

Queen of happiness, queen of light, queen of the crosses, queen of the crown(s), queen of grace in the dreaded hour of death, the pure Virgin is my protecting tree and my love.

—**Tadhg Gaelach**

NOVEMBER 20

To grow in tender love, and a respectful and sensitive charity, we have a sure Christian model to contemplate: Mary, the Mother of Jesus and our Mother, who is always attentive to the voice of God and the needs and troubles of her children.

—**Pope Francis**

FEBRUARY 12

Blessed and venerated are you, O my Lady Virgin Mary, that every faithful creature praises God for you, as you are God's most worthy creature, swift advocate obtaining forgiveness for souls.

—St. Bridget of Sweden

NOVEMBER 19

Never be afraid of loving the Blessed Virgin too much. You can never love her more than Jesus did.

—**St. Maximilian Kolbe**

FEBRUARY 13

Mary attests that the mercy of the Son of God knows no bounds and extends to everyone, without exception.

—**Pope Francis**

NOVEMBER 18

It is not enough to stop at believing that God loves us. Mary teaches us that it is necessary to respond to God-Love by loving in return. . . . To love God means to do God's will. Not one's own will but God's.

—**Chiara Lubich**

O Mary,
Mother of Mercy,
watch over all people,
that the Cross of Christ
may not be emptied of its power,
that man may . . . put his hope ever more fully in God
who is "rich in mercy" (Ephesians 2:4).

—Pope St. John Paul II

NOVEMBER 17

Mary is our advocate, the Mother of grace and mercy. She is not ungrateful towards her servants; she never forgets and always rewards them.

—St. Catherine of Siena

The faithful relate to Mary as someone by whom we find ourselves affected absolutely, as an ultimate source of comfort, grace, and salvation.

—**Leonardo Boff**

NOVEMBER 16

She is like a fiery chariot because she conceived within her the Word, the only-begotten Son of God. She carries and spreads the fire of love because her Son is love.

—**St. Catherine of Siena**

FEBRUARY 16

H ail, O torrent of compassion,
Mother of God and mother of forgiveness. . . .
You are indulgent and merciful,
dear to God, beloved above all.

—St. Ildefonsus of Toledo

NOVEMBER 15

May the Virgin Mary, perfect creation of the Trinity, help us to make our whole lives, in small gestures and more important choices, a homage to God, who is Love.

—**Pope Francis**

FEBRUARY 17

Everything in Mary derives from a sovereign grace. All that is granted to her is not due to any claim of merit, but only to God's free and gratuitous choice.

—**Pope St. John Paul II**

NOVEMBER 14

Grant, most tender of mothers, that I may be a child after your own heart and that of your divine Son.

—St. Bernadette Soubirous

FEBRUARY 18

In the conception of Mary, it was as if divine mercy and divine justice were running side by side. . . . Mercy outran justice and reached Mary sooner, because God by his very nature is much quicker at showing mercy than justice.

—St. Lawrence of Brindisi

NOVEMBER 13

The Virgin's initiative [to go to Elizabeth] was one of genuine charity; it was humble and courageous. ... Those who love forget about themselves and place themselves at the service of their neighbor.

—Pope Benedict XVI

FEBRUARY 19

She speaks today to the human heart; she proposes that . . . we do as she has done and put God in the first place in our hearts.

—**Chiara Lubich**

NOVEMBER 12

Mary is a woman who loves. How could it be otherwise? As a believer who in faith thinks with God's thoughts and wills with God's will, she cannot fail to be a woman who loves.

—**Pope Benedict XVI**

M ary understands well the reality of our life on earth, as well as the life that opens to the future and lasts forever.

—**Chiara Lubich**

NOVEMBER 11

The Holy Virgin made of her existence an unceasing and beautiful gift to God because she loved the Lord.

—Pope Francis

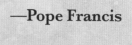

FEBRUARY 21

She is always Mother of God, she is always Mary, yet she is, so to speak, "inculturated": she has her face, her own special countenance . . . in all the countries of the earth.

—Pope Benedict XVI

NOVEMBER 10

Mary's example is an incentive . . . for all of us to live in charity for our neighbor, not out of some sort of social duty, but beginning from the love of God, from the charity of God.

—**Pope Francis**

W e will never be able to go deeply enough into the stupendous fact of what God has accomplished in Mary!

—**Pope St. Paul VI**

NOVEMBER 9

Mary is the fruit and sign of the love God has for us, of his tenderness and mercy.

—Pope Benedict XVI

FEBRUARY 23

He who is not struck by the Virgin's spirit and who does not admire her soul is ignorant of how great God is.

—**St. Peter Chrysologus**

NOVEMBER 8

Everything that she received through pure grace, Mary obtains for us and bequeaths on us. . . . She is—actively and gently, humanly and divinely— our mother.

—J. H. Nicolas

FEBRUARY 24

Dearest Mother, how happy was my soul those heavenly moments when I gazed upon you. How I love to remember those sweet moments spent in your presence, your eyes filled with kindness and mercy for us!

—**St. Bernadette Soubirous**

NOVEMBER 7

Divine Love found perfect correspondence in her, and in her womb the Only-begotten Son was made man.

—Pope Benedict XVI

Mary is the one who has the deepest knowledge of the mystery of God's mercy.

—Pope St. John Paul II

NOVEMBER 6

I n Our Lady God fell in love with humanity.

—Caryll Houselander

FEBRUARY 26

Mary appears as the one who attracts sinners and reveals to them, with her sympathy and her indulgence, the divine offer of reconciliation.

—**Pope St. John Paul II**

NOVEMBER 5

The mother is the one who gives life but also who helps and teaches how to live. Mary is a Mother, the Mother of Jesus, to whom she gave her blood and her body. And it is she who presents to us the eternal Word of the Father, who came to dwell among us.

—Pope Benedict XVI

FEBRUARY 27

She is a ship of treasures, bringing to the poor the riches of heaven.

—St. Ephrem the Syrian

NOVEMBER 4

Mary is the image and model of all mothers, of their great mission to be guardians of life, of their mission to be teachers of the art of living and of the art of loving.

—**Pope Benedict XVI**

FEBRUARY 28

Our Lady said yes for the human race. Each one of us must echo that yes for our own lives.

We are all asked if we will surrender what we are, our humanity, our flesh and blood, to the Holy Spirit and allow Christ to fill the emptiness formed by the particular shape of our life.

—Caryll Houselander

NOVEMBER 3

Madonna and Child with Two Angels
Fra Filippo Lippi

March

Her very image is as a book in which we may read at a glance the mystery of the Incarnation and the mercy of the Redemption.

—**Blessed John Henry Newman**

NOVEMBER 2

She is the very fabric of our lives. Her fiat is our fiat. But we are not stupid enough to think that she only said one fiat. She said thousands.

—**Catherine de Hueck Doherty**

MARCH 1

When I think of angels,
  Of prophets and apostles,
Of victorious martyrs,
And of the most chaste of virgins,
No one seems more powerful,
No one more merciful . . .
Than the mother of God.

—Eleventh-century prayer from northern France

All Saints' Day
NOVEMBER 1

Mary, woman of listening, open our ears; grant us to know how to listen to the word of your Son Jesus among the thousands of words of this world; grant that we may listen to the reality in which we live, to every person we encounter, especially those who are poor, in need, in hardship.

—**Pope Francis**

MARCH 2

The Virgin Annunciate
Pompeo Batoni

November

Direct your gaze to the Virgin Mary and from her "yes," learn also to pronounce your "yes" to the divine call. The Holy Spirit enters into our lives in the measure in which we open our hearts with our "yes."

—Pope Benedict XVI

MARCH 3

When we beg Mary to "pray for us sinners now and at the hour of our death," we prepare to receive the fulfillment of Mary's joy: seeing God face to face.

—**Romanus Cessario**

OCTOBER 31

"*Full of grace*" . . . is Mary's most beautiful name, the name God himself gave to her to indicate that she has always been and will always be the *beloved*, the elect, the one chosen to welcome the most precious gift, Jesus.

—Pope Benedict XVI

MARCH 4

Hail, Mary, full of grace, the Lord is with you; blessed are you among women, and blessed is the fruit of your womb, Jesus.
Holy Mary, Mother of God, pray for us sinners now and at the hour of our death. Amen.

OCTOBER 30

She was consenting not only to bear her own child, Christ, but to bear Christ into the world in all men, in all lives, in all times.

—**Caryll Houselander**

MARCH 5

The special fullness of the Holy Spirit in Mary also includes a "fullness of prayer." Through this singular fullness, Mary prays "for us"—and she prays "with us."

—Pope St. John Paul II

OCTOBER 29

Mary's yes is above all a grace. It is not simply her human response to God's offer; it is such a grace that it is at the same time the divine response to the whole of her life. It is a response of grace in her spirit to the grace established from the beginning of her life.

—**Adrienne von Speyr**

MARCH 6

May the prayer of the Mother of God come to the aid of your people, O Lord, that we may experience her intercession for us in heavenly glory.

—**Nineteenth-century prayer**

OCTOBER 28

A ve Maria! 'tis the hour of prayer!
Ave Maria! 'tis the hour of love!
Ave Maria! may our spirits dare
Look up to thine and to thy Son's above!
Ave Maria!

—**Lord Byron**

MARCH 7

O pure spouse, bearer of peace,
O Virgin and mother of the Word,
O Mary, O Mother of God;
plead with Christ for us, that he may show mercy
and intercede for our protection.

—Ninth-century Coptic prayer

OCTOBER 27

I t is easier to depict the sun with its light and its heat, Than to tell the story of Mary in its splendor.

—Jacob of Serug

MARCH 8

If I were to pray to all the saints in heaven, O mother of Jesus, . . . you are given to us to protect us.

—*Lucerna Fidelium*, **an Irish devotional**

OCTOBER 26

From Mary we learn to surrender to God's will in all things. From Mary we learn to trust even when all hope seems gone.

—**Pope St. John Paul II**

MARCH 9

She teaches us to pray: not by seeking to assert before God our own will and our own desires . . . but rather to bring them before him and let him decide what he intends to do.

—Pope Benedict XVI

OCTOBER 25

O how wondrous is Your love!
You gazed on your fairest daughter
As an eagle focuses its eye upon the sun;
You, the eternal Father, saw
her radiance,
and the Word became flesh in her.

—St. Hildegard of Bingen

MARCH 10

Mary, knowing what it is to suffer, is ever ready to administer consolation.

—St. Ignatius of Antioch

OCTOBER 24

"Hail, favored one! The Lord is with you." But she was greatly troubled at what was said and pondered what sort of greeting this might be.

—Luke 1:28-29

MARCH 11

The history of the Church teaches us that the greatest saints are those who professed the greatest devotion to Mary.

—St. John Bosco

OCTOBER 23

"The holy Spirit will come upon you, and the power of the Most High will overshadow you. Therefore the child to be born will be called holy, the Son of God."

—Luke 1:35

MARCH 12

Let us always remember that in heaven Mary prays for us, and let us therefore rely with confidence on her powerful intercession, with the desire that God's will may be done for us.

—Pope St. John Paul II

OCTOBER 22

"**B**ehold, I am the handmaid of the Lord. May it be done to me according to your word."

—**Luke 1:38**

MARCH 13

The entire body of the faithful pours forth instant supplications to the Mother of God and Mother of men that she, who aided the beginnings of the Church by her prayers, may now, exalted as she is above all the angels and saints, intercede before her Son in the fellowship of all the saints.

—*Lumen Gentium*

OCTOBER 21

The surrender that is asked of us includes complete and absolute trust; it must be like Our Lady's surrender, without condition and without reservation.

—Caryll Houselander

MARCH 14

Mary's life is as powerful an evocation of what it can mean to be God's chosen as the life of Moses, or St. Paul.

—Kathleen Norris

She was full of grace from God which was more exalted than all; the Only-begotten dwelt in her womb to renew all.

—**Jacob of Serug**

MARCH 15

Permit, O Lord, that the divine mysteries, which you have graciously established for our restoration, may, through the intercession of the ever Blessed Virgin Mary, contribute to our peace here and to our eternal salvation hereafter.

—Nineteenth-century prayer

OCTOBER 19

*H*ail, then, O full of grace!
You are the delight of him who has created
you. . . .
You are the delight of those who rejoice in the
beauty of the soul.

—St. Gregory of Nyssa

MARCH 16

By the merits, most beloved lady,
beseech your son, who takes away
all the sin that we have committed
with sweet and gracious prayer.

—**Stabat Mater**

OCTOBER 18

The Lord is with you!
    He is in you and in every place,
he is with you and of you. . . .
The Son in the bosom of his Father,
the Only Begotten Son in your womb,
the Lord, in the way known alone to him,
all in everyone
and all in you!   **–St. Gregory of Nyssa**

MARCH 17

Let us run to Mary and, as her little children, cast ourselves into her arms with a perfect confidence.

—St. Francis de Sales

OCTOBER 17

*B*lessed are you among women!
... For you have received within you the One
who is so great
that nothing in the world could him contain,
you have received him who fills all with himself,
for you have become the place
in which has come to pass salvation.

–St. Gregory of Nyssa

MARCH 18

Mary is the great Virgin in prayer, and she lifts up her hands in a gesture of openness to God and of universal supplication, concerned in a motherly fashion for the salvation of all.

—Pope St. John Paul II

OCTOBER 16

We acknowledge your great and loving purpose
in committing the honor of Mary, virgin
Mother of God,
into the care of Saint Joseph, righteous and faithful,
and placing under his watchful protection
your only Son our Savior Jesus Christ.

**—Eucharistic Preface in the
Ambrosian Liturgy**

St. Joseph, husband of Mary
MARCH 19

By your tender love for your Son,
by the glories you have received
from the Most Holy Trinity,
do not reject me from your service
but as my sovereign and my queen
preside over all my actions.

—St. Bartolome de los Rios

OCTOBER 15

Our Lady was full of God because she lived for God alone, yet she thought of herself only as the handmaid of the Lord. Let us do the same.

—St. Teresa of Calcutta

MARCH 20

In Mary is perfectly realized God's whole creative and redemptive plan. That is why she is said to be for us a light of truth and a pattern of life.

—**Thomas Merton**

OCTOBER 14

As Mary listened to the voice of an angel, may you be open to God's voice and respond to God's will each day of your life. Amen.

—*Solemn Blessing*

MARCH 21

While nourished with the comforting food of heaven, we implore your mercy, O Lord, that we, being strengthened by the powerful prayers of the Blessed Virgin Mary, may never through any temptation be separated from you.

–Nineteenth-century Eucharistic Prayer

OCTOBER 13

As for the feast of the Annunciation, the church celebrates it on whichever day of the week the 25th falls: even if it falls on Good Friday, we will still celebrate the liturgy, since the Annunciation is the beginning and source of all other feasts.

—Syriac Orthodox calendar,
seventeenth century

MARCH 22

O happy Mary, O glorious Virgin, grant me the sight of your most renowned household; grant me light of Light and the sight of the Trinity and the grace of patience against adversity.

—Nineteenth-century Irish poem

OCTOBER 12

Her response of faith included both perfect cooperation with "the grace of God" . . . and perfect openness to the action of the Holy Spirit.

—Pope St. John Paul II

MARCH 23

The Rosary . . . is the prayer for all human beings in the world and in history, living or dead, called to be in the Body of Christ and to become with Him coheirs of the glory of the Father.

—Pope St. John Paul II

OCTOBER 11

Mary is asked to assent to a truth never expressed before. She accepts it with a simple yet daring heart.

—**Pope St. John Paul II**

MARCH 24

The prayer of the Rosary is the prayer of people for people. It is the prayer of human solidarity, the collegial prayer of the redeemed, which reflects the spirit and intentions of the first redeemed person, Mary, Mother and image of the Church.

—Pope St. John Paul II

OCTOBER 10

One humble daughter of poor folk and one angel met each other and spoke of a wonderful tale.

A pure virgin and a fiery Watcher spoke with wonder: a discourse which reconciled dwellers of earth and heaven.

—**Jacob of Serug**

Annunciation
MARCH 25

Whenever we say the rosary, the joyful mysteries thus place us once more before the inexpressible event which is at the center and summit of history: the coming on earth of Emmanuel, God with us.

—**Pope St. Paul VI**

OCTOBER 9

Her "let it be" is a full and free acceptance of the will of God based entirely on simple trust in that God.

—Tim Perry and Daniel Kendall

MARCH 26

The orderly and gradual unfolding of the Rosary reflects the very way in which the Word of God, mercifully entering into human affairs, brought about the Redemption. . . .

. . . The succession of Hail Mary's constitutes the warp on which is woven the contemplation of the mysteries.

—Pope St. Paul VI

OCTOBER 8

"Mary kept all these things, pondering them in her heart" (Luke 2:19) . . . The Greek verb used . . . means "put together" and makes us think of a great mystery that must be discovered little by little.

—Pope Benedict XVI

MARCH 27

Who could have given me Our Lord, but the Virgin Mary? It was easy to pray to her, repetitious though it may seem. Saying the rosary as I did so often, I felt that I was praying with the people of God, who held on to the physical act of the rosary as to a lifeline.

—Dorothy Day

Our Lady of the Rosary
OCTOBER 7

Only by the power of the Holy Spirit, who "overshadowed" her, was Mary able to accept what is "impossible with men, but not with God" (cf. Mark 10:27).

—**Pope St. John Paul II**

MARCH 28

How entirely blessed was the mind of the Virgin which, through the indwelling and guidance of the Spirit, was always and in every way open to the power of the Word of God.

—St. Lawrence Justinian

OCTOBER 6

The event of the Annunciation is the paradigm for any act of grace: the initiative and the act . . . belong totally to God, yet the human response is equally essential.

—**Denis Farkasfalvy, OCist**

MARCH 29

Ounique mother and virgin Mary, intercede for me. O most merciful one, by whom is saved the whole world, so that, saved by your merits, O most splendid virgin, I may reach the eternal kingdom.

—Ninth-century Irish prayer

OCTOBER 5

In surrendering to the Spirit and becoming the Bride of Life, she wed God to the human race and made the whole world pregnant with the life of Christ.

—**Caryll Houselander**

MARCH 30

H ail, O Lady,
Mary, holy Mother of God:
you are the Virgin made Church
and the one . . .
in whom there was and is
the fullness of grace and every good.

—St. Francis of Assisi

OCTOBER 4

Let us look above all at Mary. At her school, we too, like her, can experience that "yes" of God to humanity from which flow all the "yeses" of our life.

—Pope Benedict XVI

MARCH 31

Let us ask the Virgin Mary to teach us the secret of silence that becomes praise, of recollection that is conducive to meditation, of love for nature that blossoms in gratitude to God.

—Pope Benedict XVI

OCTOBER 3

Madonna on a Crescent Moon

April

The Virgin is the One who continues to listen, always ready to do the Lord's will; she is an example for the believer who lives in search of God.

—Pope Benedict XVI

OCTOBER 2

The Virgin Mary . . . is held up as an example to the faithful . . . because she heard the word of God and acted on it, and because charity and a spirit of service were the driving force of her actions. She is worthy of imitation because she was the first and most perfect of Christ's disciples.

—**Pope St. Paul VI**

APRIL 1

Mother of truth, you have excelled everyone; pray with me to your Firstborn that He save me at judgement.

—**St. Columcille of Iona**

"But Mary treasured all these words and pondered them in her heart" (Luke 2:19)....

She kept silent because the two could not speak at once. The word must always rest against silence, like a painting against a background.

—**Chiara Lubich**

APRIL 2

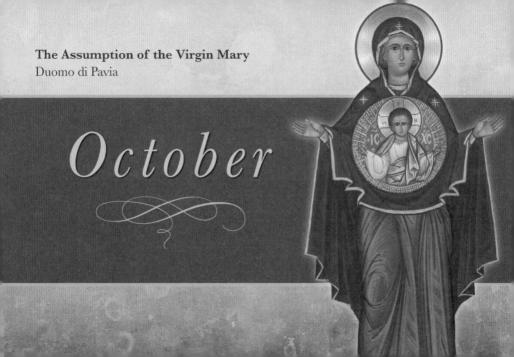

The Assumption of the Virgin Mary
Duomo di Pavia

October

Mary . . . stands before us as a sign of comfort, encouragement and hope. She turns to us, saying: "Have the courage to dare with God! Try it! Do not be afraid of him! Have the courage to risk with faith! Have the courage to risk with goodness!" Have the courage to risk with a pure heart!

—Pope Benedict XVI

APRIL 3

The beauty of Mary is beyond measure,
because another who is greater than she has not
arisen in all the world.

—Jacob of Serug

SEPTEMBER 30

Mary's request: "Do whatever he tells you," keeps its ever timely value for Christians of every age. . . . It is an exhortation to trust without hesitation, especially when one does not understand the meaning or benefit of what Christ asks.

—Pope St. John Paul II

APRIL 4

Who is she!
Who comes forth
As the morning light
Beautiful as the moon
Bright as the sun
Terrible as an army
Set in battle array.

—Zambian prayer

SEPTEMBER 29

Our Lady knew . . . that the greatest of all griefs is to be unable to mitigate the suffering of one whom we love. But she was willing to suffer that, because that was what He asked of her.

—**Caryll Houselander**

APRIL 5

M aiden, full of beauty hidden in her and around her, and pure of heart that she might see the mysteries which had come to pass in her.

—**Jacob of Serug**

SEPTEMBER 28

Sad to my heart are the words of the woman bent over her Son. God's heart softened to her weeping; her heart was dead while He was in the grave.

—Thirteenth-century Irish poem

APRIL 6

Hail then, Star of the Sea, we joy in the recollection of you. Pray for us ever at the throne of Grace; plead our cause, pray with us, present our prayers to your Son and Lord—now and in the hour of our death, Mary be our help.

—Blessed John Henry Newman

Mary, Star of the Sea
SEPTEMBER 27

In the center of the Christian story stands not the lovely "white lady" of artistic and popular imagination, kneeling in adoration before her son. Rather, it is the young pregnant woman, living in occupied territory and struggling against victimization and for survival and dignity.

—Elizabeth Schüssler Fiorenza

APRIL 7

Jesus' masterpiece is Mary, his greatest work: she, the Father's perfect daughter, who corresponded most perfectly to grace, who took full advantage of the redemption.

—**Chiara Lubich**

SEPTEMBER 26

O holy Mother of God
who, receiving the angel's message,
conceived the Word,
you gave your consent in faith,
you begot your Son in the flesh,
deeply disturbed by the divine presence,
but trustful in the help of grace.

—Seventh-century prayer

APRIL 8

I see you in a thousand paintings
Mary, so tenderly depicted
Yet none of them can begin to show you
As my soul sees you.

—Friedrich von Hardenberg

SEPTEMBER 25

May the maiden of Nazareth, who in the whole world has assumed a thousand names and faces in order to be close to her children, intercede for all of us and help us to sing of the great works that the Lord is accomplishing in us and through us.

—**Pope Francis**

APRIL 9

Almighty God has supplied us with a bright star, fair and radiant, sitting very close to Him, that is Our Lady Saint Mary, by whose example we should guide all the course of our life.

—**Dame Eleanor Hull**

SEPTEMBER 24

Who but a strong, decisive woman would call down God's justice on the heads of the oppressors of the poor? . . . Mary's original YES finds its proper expression in her making her own divine NO to what crushes the lowly.

—Elizabeth Johnson

APRIL 10

However great be the beauty of something from God,
it is not acclaimed if freedom is not present.

The sun is beautiful but it is not praised by spectators,
because it is known that its will does not give it light.

—Jacob of Serug

SEPTEMBER 23

She is a genuine model to me now as she was not when I was young. As a pregnant mother and as witness to the cross, she testifies to the joy, the pain, and the promise of all human life. . . . Above all, she reminds me of God's insistence that all creation and every human being, no matter how poor or powerless, is truly significant.

—**Sally Cunneen**

APRIL 11

She is all beautiful, all near to God. For she, surpassing the cherubim, exalted beyond the seraphim, is placed near to God.

—**St. John Damascene**

SEPTEMBER 22

What immense strength it took to accept Gabriel's message and the long agony she knew being the mother of the chosen one would be; what fortitude and persistent courage it took to live the life that unfolded, a life of wandering, exile, danger, poverty.

—Andrew Harvey

APRIL 12

Be ever in my house, come into my heart, O noble Mary, and remain in it. If I were granted a hundred clear-speaking sages' tongues, I could not tell, O gentle Mary, your wonders.

—**Donnchadh Mór Ó Dálaigh**

SEPTEMBER 21

Mary's motherhood, which began with her *fiat* in Nazareth, is fulfilled at the foot of the Cross. . . . The maternal vocation and mission of the Virgin towards those who believe in Christ actually began when Jesus said to her: "Woman, behold your son!" (John 19:26).

—Pope Benedict XVI

APRIL 13

Her presence with the disciples in the upper room before Pentecost speaks of her ability to be there for others who were caught up in their suffering and loss.

—**Joyce Rupp**

SEPTEMBER 20

Mary is the Mother of God, our mother and mother of the Church. So many men and women, young and old, have turned to her to say "thank you" and to beg a favor.

Mary takes us to Jesus and Jesus gives us peace. Let us turn to her, trusting in her assistance, with courage and hope.

—**Pope Francis**

APRIL 14

Woman of Compassion, Mother of Sorrows,
I draw inspiration from your journey.
I, too, can move through the pain of my present situation.
Your faith and courage lead me to my own strength.

—**Joyce Rupp**

SEPTEMBER 19

Yesterday, today, and tomorrow, the image of Mary calls on us to be strong and creative in our responses to the sacred potentialities of all life.

—**Sally Cunneen**

APRIL 15

I have come to think of Mary as the patron saint of "both/and" passion over "either/or" reasoning. . . . I have learned never to discount her ability to confront and disarm the polarities that so often bring human endeavors to an impasse: the subjective and objective, the expansive and the parochial, the affective and the intellectual.

—**Kathleen Norris**

SEPTEMBER 18

Mary of Nazareth, while completely devoted to the will of God, was far from being a timidly submissive woman . . . ; on the contrary, she was a woman who did not hesitate to proclaim that God vindicates the humble and the oppressed, and removes the powerful people of this world from their privileged positions (cf. Luke 1:51-53).

—Pope St. Paul VI

APRIL 16

In order to love Mary as she deserves, I think we need to delve deeper, to understand more fully, a little better who she is.

—Chiara Lubich

SEPTEMBER 17

The modern woman will recognize in Mary, who "stands out among the poor and humble of the Lord," a woman of strength, who experienced poverty and suffering, flight and exile (cf. Matthew 2:13-23).

—Pope St. Paul VI, quoting *Lumen Gentium*

APRIL 17

For centuries she has been given the title "Mother of Sorrows" or "Our Lady of Sorrows" because of the heartaches she experienced as the mother of Jesus and because her sorrow symbolizes the many pains that continue to pierce human lives today.

—**Joyce Rupp**

SEPTEMBER 16

For a sermon on the Blessed Virgin to please me, . . . , I must see her real life. . . . They should present her as imitable, bringing out her virtues, saying that she lived by faith just like ourselves, giving proofs of this from the Gospel.

—St. Thérèse of Lisieux

APRIL 18

It is expressly noted of her that she stood by the Cross. She did not grovel in the dust, but stood upright to receive the blows, the stabs, which the long Passion of her Son inflicted upon her every moment.

—Blessed John Henry Newman

Our Lady of Sorrows
SEPTEMBER 15

Mary is the model for the basic attitude we all ought to have before God, the only attitude worthy of a creature: openness and total acceptance.

—Leonardo Boff

APRIL 19

Meditate assiduously on the mysteries of his passion and on the pains that his Blessed Mother suffered at the foot of the cross. Watch and pray at all times.

—St. Clare of Assisi

SEPTEMBER 14

Her role in the history of salvation did not end in the mystery of the Incarnation but was completed in loving and sorrowful participation in the death and Resurrection of her Son.

—Pope Benedict XVI

APRIL 20

Mary of a thousand titles, Mary my mother, teach me, teach us, faith, trust, selflessness, poverty, detachment, obedience . . . and caritas—love—your Son!

—**Catherine de Hueck Doherty**

SEPTEMBER 13

The Church above all celebrates God's wonderful deeds in Christ's Paschal Mystery and in this celebration finds Mary intimately joined to her Son.

—*Collection of Masses of the Blessed Virgin Mary*, General Introduction

APRIL 21

W ho can repeat the name of Mary without finding before them music which goes to the heart, and brings before them thoughts of God and Jesus Christ, and heaven above, and fills them with the desire of those graces by which heaven is gained?

—Blessed John Henry Newman

Holy Name of Mary
SEPTEMBER 12

The figure of the Blessed Virgin does not disillusion any of the profound expectations of the men and women of our time but offers them the perfect model of the disciple of the Lord: . . . the disciple who is the active witness of that love which builds up Christ in people's hearts.

—Pope St. Paul VI

APRIL 22

O noble Virgin, truly you are greater than any other greatness. For who is your equal in greatness, O dwelling place of God the Word? To whom among all creatures shall I compare you? . . . You are greater than them all.

—St. Athanasius

SEPTEMBER 11

Mary, Mother of God, dwelling place
of the divine benevolence, through your prayers
make of me a chosen instrument
worthy of sharing
in the holy works of your Son.

—Tenth-century prayer

APRIL 23

And since His grace is greater than that of all who are born,
the beauty of Mary shall be much extolled because
she was his mother.

—**Jacob of Serug**

SEPTEMBER 10

The ultimate purpose of devotion to the Blessed Virgin is to glorify God and to lead Christians to commit themselves to a life that is in absolute conformity with His will.

—Pope St. Paul VI

APRIL 24

Vouchsafe, O Lord, to your servants the gift of heavenly grace, that those to whom the birth of the Blessed Virgin was the beginning of salvation, may in her holy festival obtain an increase of peace.

—Nineteenth-century prayer

SEPTEMBER 9

In her, the entire Church, in its incomparable variety of life and of work, attains the most authentic form of the perfect imitation of Christ.

—Pope St. Paul VI

APRIL 25

Today the Virgin is born, tended and formed and prepared for her role as Mother of God, who is the universal King of the ages.

—**St. Andrew of Crete**

Nativity of the Virgin Mary
SEPTEMBER 8

Let us live as the Blessed Virgin lives: loving God only, desiring God only, trying to please God only in all that we do.

—St. John Vianney

APRIL 26

For in making her his Mother, he gave her at once, so to say, all that he could give of beauty and goodness and holiness and sanctity in the treasury of his omnipotence.

—St. Leonard of Port Maurice

SEPTEMBER 7

All the virtues extolled in the Gospel—faith, charity, hope, humility, mercy, purity of heart—flourished in Mary, the first and most perfect of Christ's disciples.

—*Collection of Masses of the Blessed Virgin Mary*, General Introduction

APRIL 27

God could create an infinity of suns, one more brilliant than the other, an infinity of worlds, one more marvelous than the other. . . . But a creature more holy, more ravishing, more gracious than his mother he could not make.

—St. Leonard of Port Maurice

SEPTEMBER 6

Angels and archangels may have gathered there,
Cherubim and seraphim thronged the air;
But His mother only, in her maiden bliss,
Worshipped the beloved with a kiss.

—**Christina Rossetti**

APRIL 28

My desire is for the young people of the entire world to come closer to Mary. She is the bearer of an indelible youthfulness and beauty that never wanes.

—Pope St. John Paul II

SEPTEMBER 5

Do not get discouraged when you see yourself full of defects, but go to Jesus and Mary confidently, and humble yourself without becoming discouraged; then go forward bravely.

—St. Mary Mazzarello

APRIL 29

Looking at Mary, how can we, her children, fail to let the aspiration to beauty, goodness and purity of heart be aroused in us?

—Pope Benedict XVI

SEPTEMBER 4

She turns to us, saying: . . . "Commit yourselves to God, then you will see that it is precisely by doing so that your life will become broad and light, . . . filled with infinite surprises, for God's infinite goodness is never depleted!"

—Pope Benedict XVI

APRIL 30

Now if grace is beauty of spirit, what must be Mary's beauty that surpasses all the beauty of the angels?

—**St. Lawrence of Brindisi**

SEPTEMBER 3

Russian Elousa
Marek Czarnecki

May

Mary is the epitome of beauty. Masterpieces are never partial beauties, but a synthesis of the beautiful: Mary is the creature most clearly revealing the divine Trinitarian presence.

—Pope St. Paul VI

SEPTEMBER 2

Mary, in the mystery of her annunciation and visitation, is the very model of the way we should live, because first she received Jesus in her life; then what she had received, she had to share.

—St. Teresa of Calcutta

MAY 1

For as the dawn is the end of night, and the beginning of day, well may the Blessed Virgin Mary, who was the end of vices, be called the dawn of day.

—**Pope Innocent III**

SEPTEMBER 1

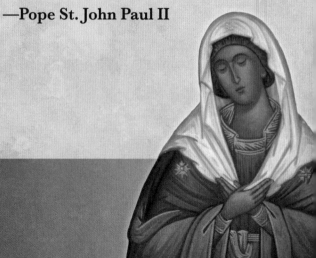

Where Mary is present, grace abounds and people are healed both in body and soul.

—Pope St. John Paul II

MAY 2

Virgin Mary
Richard Gunion

September

Mary is the image and model of all mothers, of their great mission to be guardians of life, of their mission to be teachers of the art of living and of the art of loving.

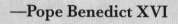

—**Pope Benedict XVI**

MAY 3

Our Lady is always close to us; she looks upon each one of us with maternal love and accompanies us always on our journey. Do not hesitate to turn to her for every need, especially when the burden of life with all its problems makes itself felt.

—Pope Francis

AUGUST 31

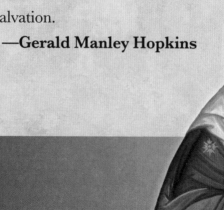

This ecstasy all through mothering earth
Tells Mary her mirth till Christ's birth
To remember and exultation
In God who was her salvation.

—Gerald Manley Hopkins

MAY 4

S ome people are so foolish that they think they can go through life without the help of the Blessed Mother.

—Padre Pio

AUGUST 30

I fervently hope that you young people will continue to press forward, not only cherishing the *memory* of the past, but also with *courage* in the present and *hope* for the future. These attitudes were certainly present in the young Mary of Nazareth.

—**Pope Francis**

MAY 5

Gentle Mary, good maiden, give us help, thou casket of the Lord's body and shrine of all mysteries.

—**St. Columcille of Iona**

AUGUST 29

L et us ask the Mother of God to obtain for us the gift of a mature faith . . . with the absolute certainty that God wants nothing but love and life, always and for everyone.

—**Pope Benedict XVI**

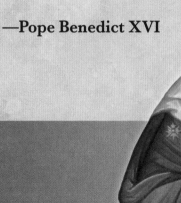

MAY 6

Thou art an invincible warrior in defense of thy servants, fighting against the devils who assail them.

—**St. Bernard of Clairvaux**

AUGUST 28

Faith is at the heart of Mary's entire story. Her song helps us to understand the mercy of the Lord as the driving force of history, the history of each of us and of all humanity.

—**Pope Francis**

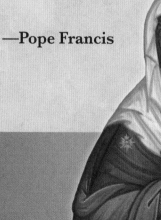

MAY 7

You know, most merciful queen, that you were born so that of you would be born, he who is God and Man, Our Lord Jesus Christ, true God and true Man, in whom I most truly believe.

—Prayer from an eleventh-century Psalter

AUGUST 27

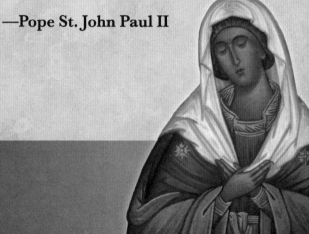

The figure of Mary shows that God has such esteem for woman that any form of discrimination lacks a theoretical basis.

—Pope St. John Paul II

MAY 8

She to whom the moon, the sun, all things,
are devoted in all time.
The moist grace of heaven
brings forth the flesh of the maiden.

—St. Fortunatus the Apostle

AUGUST 26

Let us . . . entrust ourselves to Mary, that She . . . may teach us to have the same maternal spirit toward our brothers and sisters, with the sincere capacity to welcome, to forgive, to give strength and to instill trust and hope.

—**Pope Francis**

MAY 9

The Church looks up and greets in Mary, her own model, that eternal future which in Mary has already become a present reality.

—**Karl Rahner**

AUGUST 25

She was a person of discernment, full of the love of God,

because our Lord does not dwell where there is no love.

—Jacob of Serug

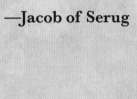

MAY 10

O Christ,
blessed is the Virgin, your Mother,
glorious queen of the world,
for, at the greeting of the angel,
she believed that which was announced
by the Lord would be accomplished.

—Seventh-century prayer

AUGUST 24

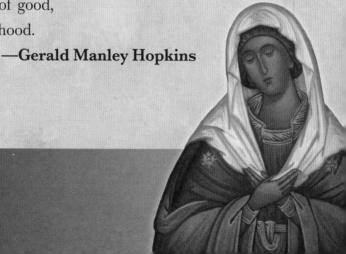

All things rising, all things sizing
Mary sees, sympathizing
With that world of good,
Nature's motherhood.

—**Gerald Manley Hopkins**

MAY 11

Most holy virgin, mother of the creator of the world, queen of high heaven, . . .
whom God chose for his mother, and who believed in his Word and conceived it, and having become pregnant gave birth to our Salvation!

—Flavius Cresconius Corippus

AUGUST 23

Devotion to Mary . . . helps us better to discern the face of a God who shares the joys and sufferings of humanity.

—Pope St. John Paul II

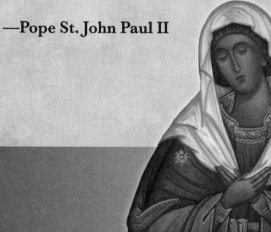

MAY 12

Y ou exalted the Mother of Christ
and crowned her in heaven with royal honors,
so that she might be a sign of your loving kindness
and a strong help for all your children.

**—Preface for the octave of the Assumption in
the Ambrosian Liturgy**

Queenship of Mary
AUGUST 22

B lessed Virgin Mary of Fatima, . . . Guard our life with your embrace:

bless and strengthen every desire for good;

give new life and nourishment to faith;

sustain and enlighten hope;

awaken and animate charity;

guide us all on the path to holiness.

—**Pope Francis**

Our Lady of Fatima
MAY 13

Has anyone ever come away from her troubled or saddened or ignorant of the heavenly mysteries?

—St. Amadeus of Lausanne

AUGUST 21

When Elizabeth heard Mary's greeting, the infant leaped in her womb, and Elizabeth, filled with the holy Spirit, cried out in a loud voice and said, "Most blessed are you among women, and blessed is the fruit of your womb."

—Luke 1:41-42

MAY 14

I am Angelic Love who wheel around
that high gladness inspired by the womb
that was the dwelling place of our Desire;
so shall I circle, Lady of Heaven, until
you, following your Son, have made that sphere
supreme, still more divine by entering it.

—Dante Alighieri

AUGUST 20

"And how does this happen to me, that the mother of my Lord should come to me? For at the moment the sound of your greeting reached my ears, the infant in my womb leaped for joy."

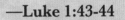

—**Luke 1:43-44**

MAY 15

She is the link that joins the four periods of salvation history. Mary belongs to the Old Testament in which she was born. She is witness to the earthly life of Christ. She is present at the birth of the Church (Acts 1:14). And, body and soul in heaven, she inaugurates the age of totally redeemed humanity.

—**Leonardo Boff**

AUGUST 19

"**B**lessed are you who believed that what was spoken to you by the Lord would be fulfilled."

—**Luke 1:45**

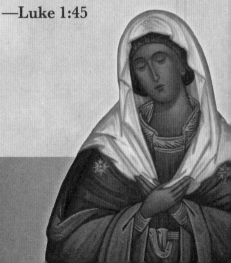

MAY 16

Because she had proved to be the most humble among angels and men, Mary was raised above all that was created, and is most beautiful of all and more like God than any other can be.

—**St. Bridget of Sweden**

AUGUST 18

The Word and the Voice were there in two wombs;
In Elizabeth there was the Voice and in Mary,
the Word. . . .

The Voice is the messenger of the Word, and his
evangelist:

He makes Him known, also showing Him forth and
extolling Him.

—Jacob of Serug

MAY 17

Today the Virgin Mary begs the height of heaven;
The heavenly host rejoices and we all rejoice in God,
Giving thanks to her, of whom he was honored to be born,
Celebrating the feast day for the honor of the Virgin Mary
Who deserved to ascend to heavenly realms.
Of whose Assumption angels rejoice
And extol the Son of God.

**—Twelfth-century introit antiphon
for the Assumption**

AUGUST 17

If you meet the Virgin on the road, invite her into your house. She bears the word of God.

—St. John of the Cross

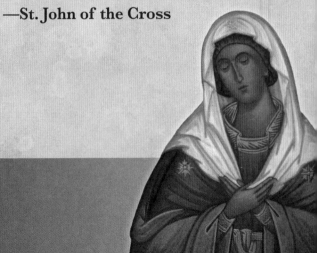

MAY 18

Betrothed with the dowry of faith, made holy by her virtues,
The Bride is crowned and united with God, the Bridegroom.

—Twelfth-century inscription

AUGUST 16

The Magnificat . . . is entirely woven from threads of Holy Scripture, threads drawn from the Word of God. . . . she speaks and thinks with the Word of God; the Word of God becomes her word, and her word issues from the Word of God.

—Pope Benedict XVI

MAY 19

Mary's Assumption shows us our own destiny as God's adoptive children and members of the body of Christ. Like Mary our Mother, we are called to share fully in the Lord's victory over sin and death, and to reign with him in his eternal Kingdom. This is our vocation.

—**Pope Francis**

Assumption of the Blessed Virgin Mary
AUGUST 15

In line with the great biblical singers Miriam, Deborah, and Hannah, Mary praises God. This prayer [the Magnificat] is the longest set of words placed on the lips of any woman in the New Testament.

—**Elizabeth Johnson**

MAY 20

Today the Virgin Mother of Christ
was taken up into the heavens,
to be the beginning and likeness
of your Church in its fullness
and an assurance of hope and consolation
for your people on their pilgrim way.

—Preface for the Feast of the Assumption

AUGUST 14

Mary inherits the faith of her people and shapes it into a song that is entirely her own, yet at the same time is the song of the entire Church, which sings it with her.

—**Pope Francis**

MAY 21

Whatever you wish
Your only son will give you.
For whomever you seek
You will have pardon and glory.

—Eleventh-century poem from
northern France

AUGUST 13

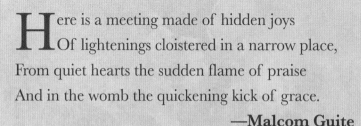

Here is a meeting made of hidden joys
Of lightenings cloistered in a narrow place,
From quiet hearts the sudden flame of praise
And in the womb the quickening kick of grace.

—**Malcom Guite**

MAY 22

Holy Mary, succor the wretched,
help the disheartened,
put new heart into the feeble.
Pray for the people, intervene for the clergy,
intercede for all holy women.
May all those who honor your memory
experience your generous help.

—St. Fulbert of Chartres

AUGUST 12

Two women on the very edge of things
  Unnoticed and unknown to men of power,
But in their flesh the hidden Spirit sings
And in their lives the buds of blessing flower.

—Malcom Guite

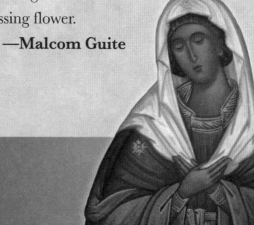

MAY 23

Take shelter under Our Lady's mantle, and do not fear. She will give you all you need. She is very rich, and besides is very generous with her children. She loves giving.

—**St. Raphaela Maria**

AUGUST 11

And Mary stands with all we call "too young,"
Elizabeth with all called "past their prime."
They sing today for all the great unsung,
Women who turned eternity to time,
Favoured of heaven, outcast on the earth,
Prophets who bring the best in us to birth.

—**Malcom Guite**

MAY 24

Mary was the first person to take the "way" to enter the Kingdom of God that Christ opened, a way which is accessible to the humble, to all who trust in the word of God and endeavor to put it into practice.

—Pope Benedict XVI

AUGUST 10

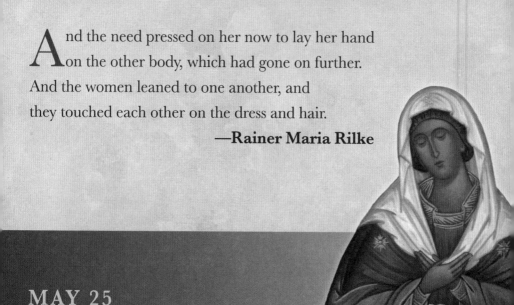

And the need pressed on her now to lay her hand
on the other body, which had gone on further.
And the women leaned to one another, and
they touched each other on the dress and hair.

—Rainer Maria Rilke

MAY 25

Mary, Mother of Grace,
Mother of mercy,
Shield me from the enemy
And receive me at the hour of my death. Amen.

—Twelfth-century Irish prayer

AUGUST 9

Reading the Magnificat, we realize how well Mary knew the word of God. Every verse of her song has a parallel in the Old Testament. The young mother of Jesus knew the prayers of her people by heart.

—**Pope Francis**

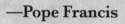

MAY 26

Heaven and earth will pass away before Mary would abandon a soul.

—Blessed Henry Suso

AUGUST 8

L et Mary's soul be in each of you to proclaim the greatness of God.

—St. Ambrose

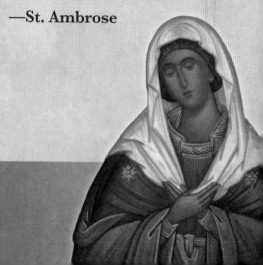

MAY 27

Who can accompany us better on this demanding journey of holiness than Mary? Who can teach us to adore Christ better than she? May she help especially the new generations to recognize the true face of God in Christ and to worship, love, and serve him with total dedication.

—Pope Benedict XVI

AUGUST 7

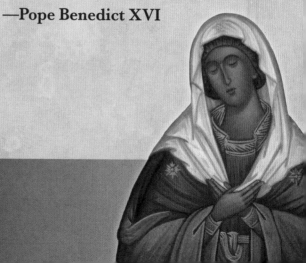

Mary's greatness consists in the fact that she wants to magnify God, not herself.

—Pope Benedict XVI

MAY 28

But oh! Queen of all grace and counsel,
Cause of our joy, Oh Clement Virgin, come:
Show us those eyes as chaste as lightning,
Kinder than June and true as Scripture.
Heal with your looks the poisons of the universe,
And claim your Son's regenerate world!

—Thomas Merton

AUGUST 6

Mary's is a revolutionary prayer, the song of a faith-filled young woman conscious of her limits yet confident in God's mercy.

—Pope Francis

MAY 29

Amid all the ranks of the saints, the first place for humility, purity and tender love is held by the blessed virgin, the mother of Jesus.

—**John of Forde**

Dedication of the
Basilica of St. Mary Major
AUGUST 5

Mary's visit to Elizabeth, in fact, is a prelude to Jesus' mission and, in cooperating from the beginning of her motherhood in the Son's redeeming work, she becomes the model for those in the Church who set out to bring Christ's light and joy to the people of every time and place.

—Pope St. John Paul II

MAY 30

For so great is her dignity, so great her favor before God, that whosoever in his need will not have recourse to her is trying to fly without wings.

—**Pope Leo XIII**

AUGUST 4

"My soul proclaims the greatness of the Lord;
my spirit rejoices in God my savior.
For he has looked upon his handmaid's lowliness;
behold, from now on will all ages call me blessed.
The Mighty One has done great things for me,
and holy is his name."

—Luke 1:46-49

The Visitation
MAY 31

With my soul, with my body, with my understanding, and with my sense, I am under your protection as long as I may be here. . . . O Mary, hear my cry to holy heaven so that you may be my shelter against the host of base devils.

—Ninth-century Irish poem

AUGUST 3

The Virgin
Joseph Stella

June

How much we can learn from our Lady! She was so humble because she was all for God. She was full of grace. She made use of the almighty power that was in her: the grace of God.

—**St. Teresa of Calcutta**

AUGUST 2

Come, Holy Spirit. . . . Come! As you descended upon Mary that the Word might become flesh, work in us through grace as you worked in her through nature and grace.

—**St. Mary Magdalene de Pazzi**

U nder your mercy we take refuge, O Mother of God. Do not reject our supplications in necessity, but deliver us from danger, [O you] alone pure and alone blessed.

—*Sub Tuum Praesidium*

AUGUST 1

For our God Jesus Christ, according to God's economy, was conceived by Mary of the seed of David (cf. John 7:42; Romans 3:27), but also by the Holy Spirit. He was born and baptized, that by his Passion he might purify the water.

—St. Ignatius of Antioch

JUNE 2

Immaculate Heart of Mary
Cameron Smith

August

The Virgin Mary teaches us what it means to live in the Holy Spirit and what it means to accept the news of God in our life.

—**Pope Francis**

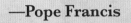

JUNE 3

M ay the Blessed Virgin revive in us the ardent "desire to live in grace," to persevere in the grace of God.

—Pope St. John Paul II

JULY 31

She conceived Jesus by the work of the Holy Spirit, and every Christian, each one of us, is called to accept the Word of God, to accept Jesus inside of us and then to bring him to everyone.

—**Pope Francis**

JUNE 4

Sweet Mary, mother of Christ,
bright flower, and maid from whom the King came,
weld in our hearts forever without wrinkle
the grace of that child, who suffered the passion on our
behalf. May it not leave us.

—Liam Rua Mac Coitir

JULY 30

The Flesh born of Mary, coming from the Holy Spirit, is Bread descended from heaven.

—St. Hilary of Poitiers

JUNE 5

God's grace and man's free will corresponding with it . . . , we . . . find its ideal illustration in the life of our Lady herself.

—Ronald A. Knox

JULY 29

She desires to form her Only-begotten in all her sons by adoption.

—**Blessed Guerric of Igny**

JUNE 6

The Mother of Christ, especially in liturgical services, shines radiantly as the "exemplar of the virtues" and of faithful cooperation in the work of salvation.

—*Collection of Masses of the Blessed Virgin Mary*

JULY 28

Where Mary is, there is the archetype of total self-giving and Christian discipleship. Where Mary is, there is the pentecostal breath of the Holy Spirit; there is new beginning and authentic renewal.

—**Pope Benedict XVI**

JUNE 7

Unfailing, beautiful mother of the holy Child, who redeemed the human race with love and joy; O pious, charitable, pondering, sweet (mother), liberate us for ever under your blessed bright mantle, O Mary of the only Son.

—Tadhg Gaelach Ó Súilleabháin

Glory of virgins, the joy of mothers, the support of the faithful, the diadem of the Church, the model of the true Faith, the seat of piety, the dwelling place of the Holy Trinity.

—St. Proclus of Constantinople

JUNE 8

Just as Mary's unique vocation found fulfillment, so—we trust the unique life of each one of us will be fulfilled.

—Elzbieta Adamiak

JULY 26

The Virgin Mary, among all creatures, is a masterpiece of the Most Holy Trinity. In her humble heart full of faith, God prepared a worthy dwelling place for himself in order to bring to completion the mystery of salvation.

—**Pope Benedict XVI**

JUNE 9

To glimpse Mary with the eyes of faith—to see her in the context of the human history that reveals the grace of God in space and time and that comes to fulfillment in Jesus Christ, her son—is, for Christians of both East and West, to see the love of God.

—Brian Daley

JULY 25

Let us ask Our Lady to help us rediscover the beauty of the Eucharist, to make it the center of our life, especially at Sunday Mass and in adoration.

—**Pope Francis**

JUNE 10

Whoever opens his or her heart to the Mother encounters and welcomes the Son and is pervaded by his joy.

—Pope Benedict XVI

If the Church gives birth to the members of Christ, then the Church greatly resembles Mary.

—St. Augustine of Hippo

JUNE 11

She should be, and herself gladly would be, the foremost example of the grace of God, to incite all the world to trust in this grace and to love and praise it.

—**Martin Luther**

JULY 23

Consider this great mystery! The Son of God has passed whole and entire, from the heart of the Father to the womb of Mary and from the womb of the Mother to the lap of the Church.

—**St. Peter Damian**

JUNE 12

Mary's *fiat* to the invitation of the Most High sprang from a radical freedom in which she surrendered to the loving will of God with a total consent of her will. An act of freedom, not coercion or violence, stands at the beginning of the new history of God-with-us.

—Leonardo Boff

JULY 22

There is an indissoluble link between the Mother and the Son generated in her womb by the work of the Holy Spirit, and this link we perceive in a mysterious way in the Sacrament of the Eucharist.

—Pope Benedict XVI

JUNE 13

Let us ask Mary to teach us how to become, like her, inwardly free, so that in openness to God we may find true freedom, true life, genuine and lasting joy.

—Pope Benedict XVI

JULY 21

She ... became the Mother of God, the image and model of the Church, chosen among the peoples to receive the Lord's blessing and communicate it to the entire human family.

—**Pope Benedict XV**

JUNE 14

By her words and her silence, the Virgin Mary stands before us as a model for our pilgrim way.

—Pope St. John Paul II

JULY 20

The ox-eyed land,
The muted lakes,
The cloudy groves that praise you,
Lady, with their blooms,
Fuse and destroy their lights
And burn them into gold for you, great Virgin,
Coining your honor in the glorious sun.

—Thomas Merton

JUNE 15

Mary wanted God to be great in the world, great in her life and present among us all.

—Pope Benedict XVI

JULY 19

Mary . . . teaches us to live "eucharistically," that is, to learn how to give thanks and praise, and not to fixate on our problems and difficulties alone. In the process of living, today's prayers become tomorrow's reasons for thanksgiving.

—**Pope Francis**

JUNE 16

For what is conversion but the *fiat* of Our Lady echoed again and the conception of Christ in yet another heart?

—**Caryll Houselander**

JULY 18

How can I live Mary, how can my life be perfumed by her beauty? By silencing the creature in me, and upon this silence, letting the Spirit of the Lord speak.

—**Chiara Lubich**

JUNE 17

Y ou chose her before all other women
    to be for your people an advocate of grace
and a pattern of holiness.

—Preface in the Ambrosian Liturgy

JULY 17

In the Heart of the Redeemer we adore God's love for humanity, his will for universal salvation, his infinite mercy. . . .

The heart that resembles that of Christ more than any other is without a doubt the Heart of Mary, his Immaculate Mother.

—Pope Benedict XVI

JUNE 18

Our Lady's love is like a stream that has its source in the Eternal Fountains, quenches the thirst of all, can never be drained, and ever flows back to its Source.

—**St. Margaret Bourgeoys**

Our Lady of Mount Carmel
JULY 16

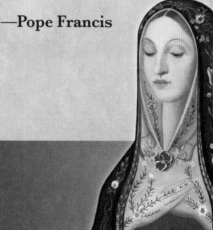

Jesus, Bread of eternal life, came down from heaven and was made flesh thanks to the faith of Mary Most Holy.

—**Pope Francis**

JUNE 19

Mary, Mother of the Lord, truly teaches us what entering into communion with Christ is: Mary offered her own flesh, her own blood to Jesus and became a living tent of the Word, allowing herself to be penetrated by his presence in body and spirit.

—Pope Benedict XVI

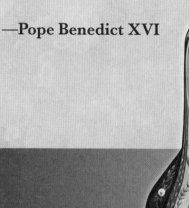

With complete availability, interior openness and freedom, she allowed God to fill her with love, with his Holy Spirit.

—Pope Benedict XVI

JUNE 20

Mary therefore is the model of our sanctification. We rejoice and are grateful to see how her life sheds so much light on our own.

—Chiara Lubich

JULY 14

Mary, the simple woman, could thus receive within herself the Son of God, and give to the world the Savior who had first given himself to her.

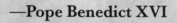

—Pope Benedict XVI

JUNE 21

God, while opening a way to sanctity, was also showing us a model we could imitate to reach it. This model was Mary.

—**Chiara Lubich**

It was precisely on Golgotha that the Redeemer, as his highest testament, established that his mother would also be the mother of all the redeemed: *Ecce Mater tua.*

—**Pope St. John XXIII**

JUNE 22

Mary lived perpetually immersed in the mystery of God-made-man, as his first and perfect disciple, by contemplating all things in her heart in the light of the Holy Spirit, in order to understand and live out the will of God.

—**Pope Francis**

JULY 12

The Blessed Virgin is the perfect realization of the Church's holiness and its model.

—Pope St. John Paul II

JUNE 23

By learning from Mary, we can understand with our hearts what our eyes and minds do not manage to perceive or contain on their own.

—**Pope Benedict XVI**

JULY 11

The words "Behold, your mother!" express Jesus' intention to inspire in his disciples an attitude of love for and trust in Mary, leading them to recognize her as their mother, the mother of every believer.

—Pope St. John Paul II

JUNE 24

Mary . . . wants to lead us toward God, to teach us a way of life in which God is acknowledged as the center of all there is and the center of our personal lives.

—Pope Benedict XVI

JULY 10

We contemplate [the Virgin Mary] in the glorious mystery of Pentecost. The Holy Spirit, who at Nazareth descended upon her to make her the Mother of the Word Incarnate (cf. Luke 1:35), descended . . . on the nascent Church joined together around her in the Upper Room (cf. Acts 1:14).

—Pope Benedict XVI

JUNE 25

Masterpiece of the Creator, . . .
Beautiful Mary!
About her we can never say enough.

—**Chiara Lubich**

The title "Mother of the Church" thus reflects the deep conviction of the Christian faithful, who see in Mary not only the mother of the person of Christ, but also of the faithful.

—**Pope St. John Paul II**

JUNE 26

Of her we do not speak, of her we sing.
Of her we do not think,
but we call upon her and love her.
She is not the subject of study, but of poetry.

—**Chiara Lubich**

She had opened the door to the Spirit and let the hearts of the coming Christ-bearers receive such gifts as fortitude, peace, patience, long-suffering, humility, and love.

—**Caryll Houselander**

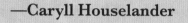

JUNE 27

This rainbow of virtue
that says "peace" to the entire world
because Peace it has given the world;
this creature, first thought of
in the mysterious abyss of the Trinity
and given to us,
was Mary.

—**Chiara Lubich**

JULY 7

The heart of Mary is visited by the grace of the Father, is permeated by the power of the Spirit and interiorly compelled by the Son; that is, we see a perfectly human heart inserted into the dynamism of the Most Holy Trinity.

—Pope Benedict XVI

JUNE 28

This marvelous shade that contains the sun,
losing and finding itself therein; . . .
was Mary.

—**Chiara Lubich**

Mother of the only begotten Son of God, Mary is Mother of the community which constitutes Christ's mystical Body and guides its first steps.

—Pope St. John Paul II

JUNE 29

In Mary we see how a truly good and provident God has established for us a most suitable example of every virtue.

—**Pope Leo XIII**

JULY 5

In contemplating her, the Church makes out her own features: Mary lives faith and charity; Mary is also a creature saved by the one Savior; Mary collaborates in the initiative of the salvation of all humanity.

—Pope Benedict XVI

JUNE 30

True freedom is found in our loving embrace of the Father's will. From Mary, full of grace, we learn that Christian freedom is more than liberation from sin. . . . It is the freedom to love God and our brothers and sisters with a pure heart, and to live a life of joyful hope for the coming of Christ's Kingdom.

—Pope Francis

JULY 4

Madonna del Libro
Sandro Botticelli

July

Only a few words from the Virgin Mary have come down to us in the Gospels. But these few words are like heavy grains of pure gold. . . . They more than suffice to bathe our entire lives in a luminous golden glow.

—St. Teresa Benedicta of the Cross

JULY 3

G od comes to us in the things we know best and can verify most easily, the things of our everyday life, apart from which we cannot understand ourselves.

—Pope St. John Paul II

JULY 1

First Mary's soul magnifies the Lord, and then, her spirit rejoices in God. Unless we first believe, we will not be able to rejoice.

—**Origen**

JULY 2